Dea
Hay

u

Rosie xx
x

C000005659

Look Up! Winchester

By Rodney Graham and Christopher Newberry

A tour of Winchester's historic High Street above the eye-line, with stories behind its façades

why **look up?**

The high streets of British cities and towns have developed over the centuries as places of trade and commerce, with the street-level shop front presenting the focus of attention to prospective customers. Most of Winchester's High Street buildings stem from the Georgian, Victorian or Edwardian periods and as such were designed as a single composition, with the shop front, defining the 'commercial waterline', and the premises above, working in architectural and functional harmony with one another. Often these buildings were erected by individuals, who wanted to stamp their 'mark' on the city. They invested a lot of money in fine architectural details in order to project their wealth and confidence in their business. It was an investment which was intended to make them the talk of the town!

Sadly, most of the original shop fronts of these fascinating buildings have disappeared. They have been replaced by unsympathetic versions that are still intended to hold our attention at street level, but which have unwittingly disconnected the compositional whole.

◀ *A time when the shop front was an integral part of the building.*

▲ *This shop near the Buttercross, is one of very few that have retained their character and where its front is still an integral part of the whole building.*

so imagine . . .

. . . that Winchester's High Street is submerged in water up to the 'commercial waterline'. All the shop fronts are under water. All we can see are the buildings above the ground floor. Your view and perception of this historic city completely changes. Even if you've lived in Winchester all your life, you would discover features of the High Street that you've probably never noticed!

Winchester has existed as an important centre of trade and commerce for a long time. Excavations along the High Street suggest that it to has the country's oldest high street. The Romans called it Venta Belgarum, the Saxons made it their capital, the Normans built its cathedral, the Georgians brought it back to prosperity, the Victorians expanded it and we neo-Elizabethans . . . well, only history will tell.

We have selected some of the less noticed buildings on Winchester's principal commercial street and look at each one as it might have appeared in the mind of its architect or designer, when it was still on the drawing board; with clean, straight lines, no perspective and no background to distract. The essence of the building.

We take you on a 'tour' of Winchester's High Street starting at what was once the Eastgate, near the bridge, and ending at the Westgate. This tour will reveal fascinating aspects of some of the buildings, presenting up close many details that we ordinarily overlook and some of the landmarks that define this historic city today.

With the help of this guide book, you can see the real Winchester when you . . .

. . . look up !

Image manipulation Khalid Saleh

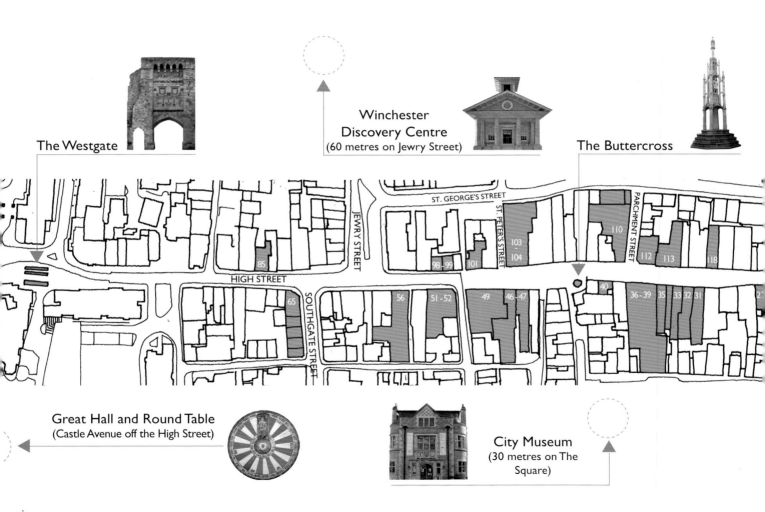

The Westgate

Winchester
Discovery Centre
(60 metres on Jewry Street)

The Buttercross

Great Hall and Round Table
(Castle Avenue off the High Street)

City Museum
(30 metres on The
Square)

ST. GEORGE'S STREET

JEWRY STREET

ST. PETER'S STREET

PARCHMENT STREET

HIGH STREET

SOUTHGATE STREET

85

103 - 104

110

112 113 118

98 - 99 101

65

56

51 - 52

49

46 - 47

40

36 - 39 35 33 32 31

The Look Up! route

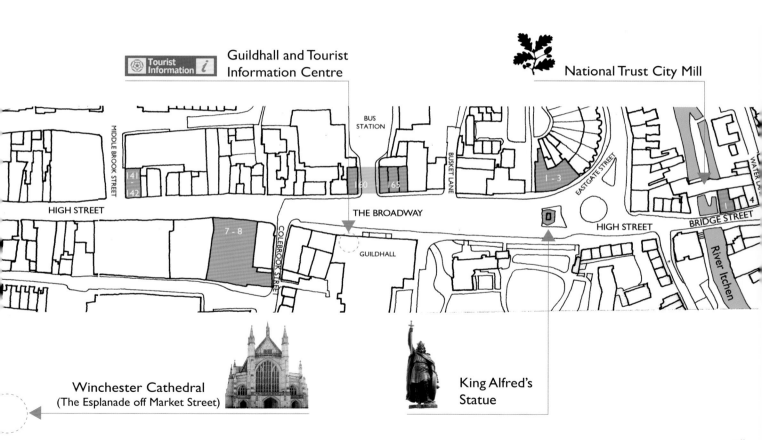

Tourist Information *i*

Guildhall and Tourist Information Centre

National Trust City Mill

BUS STATION

MIDDLE BROOK STREET

141 - 142

160 165

1 - 3

EASTGATE STREET

WATER LANE

HIGH STREET

7 - 8

COLEBROOK STREET

THE BROADWAY

GUILDHALL

HIGH STREET

BRIDGE STREET

1 4

River Itchen

Winchester Cathedral
(The Esplanade off Market Street)

King Alfred's Statue

1, Bridge Street

Built:	1602, Grade II Listed Building
Materials:	Timber frame and brick
Original purpose:	Miller's home and grain storage
Key feature:	Clay hanging tiles

Clay tiles were historically made from the same clay as bricks and used for hanging on buildings for both decorative and practical reasons - particularly to protect timber-framed buildings from fire. William Fitzstephen, a clerk in the service of Thomas Becket wrote *"A Description of The Most Noble City of London"* in about 1189: *"As for the prevention of casualties by fire, the houses in this city being then built all of timber, and covered with thatch of straw or reed, it was long since thought good policy . . . that all men in this city should build their houses of stone up to a certain height, and to cover them with slate or* **baked tile;** *since which time, thanks be given to God, there hath not happened the like often consuming fires in this city as afore."*

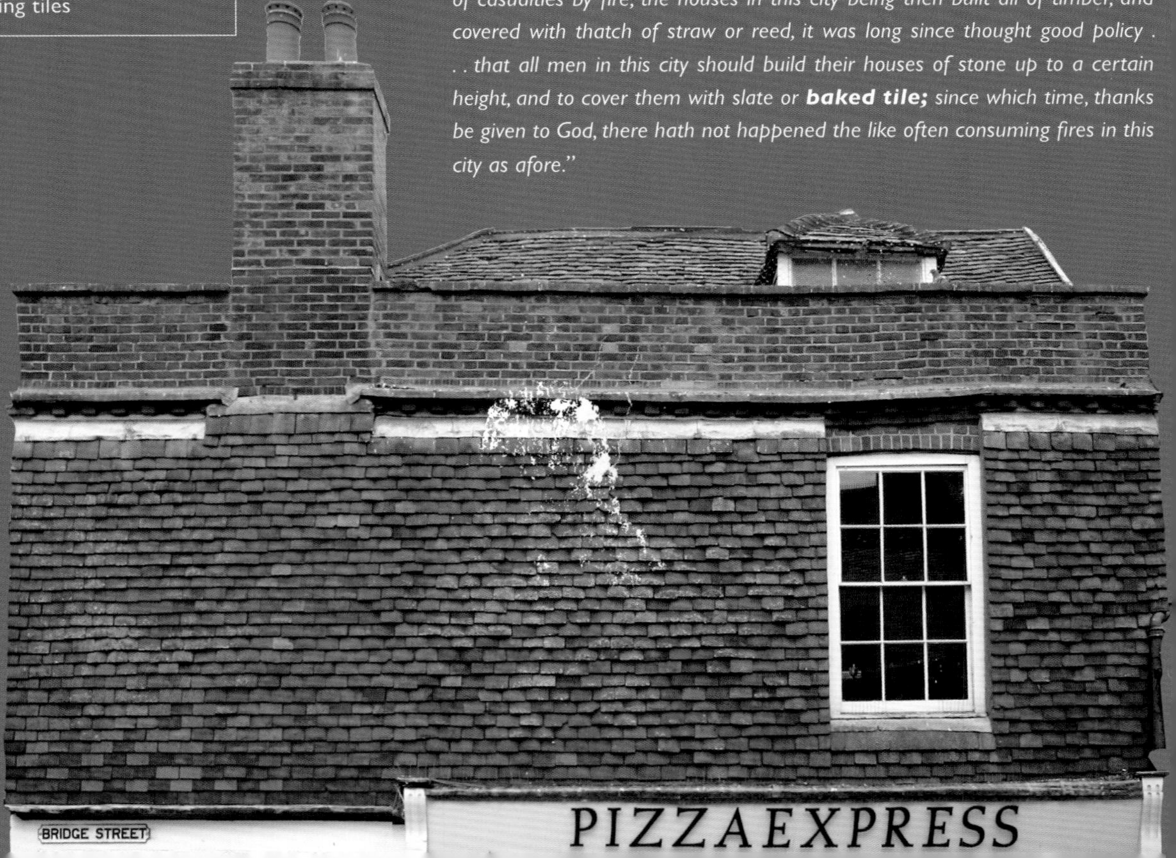

BRIDGE STREET

PIZZAEXPRESS

BRIDGE STREET

Fired clay tiles hang in a very similar way to roof shingles: An overlap of three tiles is required to ensure a watertight building envelope. ►

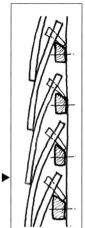

▲ *When the mill was restored in 1744, the new millrace narrowed the river to its present day width. This view of the race is taken from the back of the mill.*

There has been a bridge at this point of the River Itchen since before Roman times. In those days it was a wooden bridge, crossing a much wider river than today's. St Swithun, Bishop of Winchester, had a stone bridge built in 860 with a series of arches spanning 2 metres, reaching what is now Water Lane. The mill near the bridge was first recorded in the Domesday Book of 1086. The present building at 1, Bridge Street was constructed in the early 17th century as a granary and home for the miller. The building, together with numbers 2 - 4, Bridge Street, actually stood on the bridge, in much the same way that buildings once stood on London

Bridge. When the City Mill was rebuilt in 1744, developing the new millrace meant that the river became much narrower and in 1813 the shorter present day bridge was built.

The mill remained in use until the early 20th century when it became a laundry. It was almost demolished in 1928, but a group of benefactors intervened, buying the mill and handing it over to the National Trust, which leased the building to the Youth Hostels Association. After a standstill of almost 90 years, the mill was restored and returned to its original purpose in 2004. It is now a working mill, open to the public.

◄ *The National Trust now operates a restored working mill, open to the public with lots of information and freshly milled wholemeal flour for sale.*

1 - 3, Eastgate Street

Built: 1850, Grade II Listed Building
Materials: Render on brick
Original purpose: Part of Mildmay House redevelopment
Key feature: First plate glass window in Winchester

Glass is made of pure silica sand, soda and lime and has been made in Britain ever since Saxon times. For a long time glass was extraordinarily expensive - a great luxury! This is because it was so difficult to make: the silica sand had to be absolutely pure for the glass to be clear - even the tiniest amount of iron ore, would give it a milky grey appearance. Glass production developed over centuries. For a very long time glass was 'blown' to form large cylinders or discs from which smaller panes were cut. Then there was a breakthrough in the 1780's: when the French invented plate glass. Plate glass was produced either in cylinders or by casting, but in 1838 the process was further developed to produce large flat sheets, which allowed commercial buildings to use plate glass in their shop fronts. 3, Eastgate Street was the first shop in Winchester to have a plate glass window.

Lady Jane Mildmay (1764 - 1857) ▲

The area which now includes King Alfred's statue and Eastgate Street, including all of its buildings, was a single house, gardens and water gardens. Eastgate House, later called Mildmay House, was built in 1665 by Sir Robert Mason for Henry Penton. Sir Robert was a very well known architect at the time, who did much work for King Charles II. In 1795, being the grandest home in Winchester, it served as accommodation for King George III when he visited Winchester. Eastgate House became Mildmay House when it was purchased by Sir Henry Paulet St. John and his wife, Lady Jane Mildmay. Upon Sir Henry's death in 1808, Lady Mildmay became solely responsible for Mildmay House. She was a big landowner with many homes and by 1844 spent very little time in Winchester. She thought it best to get a valuation by Edward Driver, whose surveyor (a certain Mr. Davies) concluded that too many repairs were needed at too high a cost and recommended creating a street leading up to North Walls and dividing the land into parcels in order to *"form some very eligible and valuable sites for building and thus the attention of speculating Capitalists may be attracted"*. Which is exactly what did happen. John Cave purchased it all in 1847 and divided the land into 46 lots - including 1-3, Eastgate Street.

This rather splendid building was constructed in 1850, adding a grand sweeping entrance into Eastgate Street. The prospectus for 3, Eastgate Street (the present Chinese restaurant) stated 'premises suitable for a chemist' and is notable for being Winchester's first shop to have a plate glass window.

Charles Salter set up a catering company in 1909, which he described as "Officers' Mess Caterers and General Refreshment Contractors, etc." Later he purchased and ran the Eastgate Hotel and Restaurant at 80 Eastgate Street, (opposite 1 - 3, Eastgate Street, now an estate agents). He went on to become Mayor of Winchester. ▲

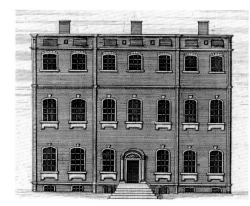

▲ *Eastgate House, later Mildmay House, was designed by Sir Robert Mason and built in 1665 - demolished in 1847.*

- Extract from William Godson's 1750 map of Winchester.

King Alfred's Statue

Erected:	1901 - Grade II Listed
Materials:	Bronze
Original purpose:	Commemoration of King Alfred's death
Key feature:	"New Sculpture" neoclassical art

Intended to commemorate one thousand years since the death of the monarch, the figure of King Alfred the Great was erected in 1901 (actually 1002 years after his death) and stands about eighteen feet high. The right hand holds his cross-hilted sword, the symbol of Christianity combating the power of heathenism. The statue was sculpted by William "Hamo" Thornycroft and erected by the Mayor of Winchester, Alfred Bowker. The word AELFRED, the King's original Saxon name, appears on the Cornish granite base. The statue was sculpted in the Victorian style of "new sculpture", a form of neoclassical art.

◀ *Engraving depicting the 'cakes episode' from "The History of Alfred the Great" by Jacob Abbott published in 1854*

King Alfred the Great was the first "King of the Anglo Saxons". He had his capital in Winchester and was largely responsible for ridding England of the Danes in the ninth century. His achievements are so much more remarkable because he started from a very weak position organising an army to repel the Danes from the isolation of a swamp in Somerset. At this point in his reign he was not yet "great" - in fact he was able to travel incognito. There is a story which is meant to underline the humility, which in the long run, brought him greatness. Alfred was given shelter by a peasant woman who didn't know who he was. She asked him to watch some cakes she was making on her griddle while she went about her daily chores. Alfred, perhaps more preoccupied with thinking of the problems of the kingdom, accidentally allowed the cakes to burn. When the woman returned and found her cakes had been burnt, she severely reprimanded the king. Later, when she found out exactly who her guest was, she pleaded for his forgiveness to which he replied that it was he who needed forgiveness for allowing her cakes to burn.

▲ *Thousands of Winchester's population attend the unveiling of King Alfred's statue in 1901*

◀ *Sir William "Hamo" Thornycroft was a very well known Victorian sculptor responsible not only for the statue of King Alfred in Winchester, but for many London landmarks including the statue of Oliver Cromwell outside the Houses of Parliament. This illustration is a cartoon published in a magazine called Vanity Fair by the famous cartoonist, Spy.*

160 - 165, High Street

Built:	1936
Materials:	Brick and cast concrete
Key feature:	Neo-Georgian

To look at these neo-Georgian buildings one would think that they were once a continuous terrace. It is very puzzling that the intended continuity of this architectural piece was interrupted: It looks as though numbers 161 - 162 were demolished to give way to the bus station and its entrance portico, but there is no record confirming the demolition. The central pediment detail to the first floor window of no. 164, which is probably manufactured as a single cement-based cast element, gives central emphasis to the composition of numbers 163 - 165, which does make one wonder whether numbers 161 - 162 ever did exist in the form suggested. It's a mystery! Architecturally speaking, despite the discontinuity of the elevation, the building is neither spectacular in its execution nor is it offensive to the eye.

WINCHESTER BUS STATION

CORAL

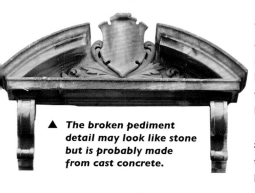

▲ **The broken pediment detail may look like stone but is probably made from cast concrete.**

The arrival of public transport - particularly the omnibus - put a lot of pressure on Winchester's old medieval streets. The Broadway had traditionally been the omnibuses' pick-up point but by 1935 this was causing havoc. Something had to be done. Part of the splendid building that was numbers 160 - 165, High Street had to go: numbers 161 and 162, High Street were apparently demolished to create the entrance to the Hampshire and Dorset Omnibus Company's terminal.

Winchester Bus Station in the early sixties ▲

7 - 8, High Street

Built:	1871
Materials:	Brick and cast reconstituted stone
Original purpose:	Purveyors of china and glass
Key feature:	Palladian influence

C & H

C & H

C & H

C & H fabrics

16

The design of this building is clearly influenced by Palladian architecture, named after Andrea Palladio *(see right),* one of the most influential architects of all time and responsible for many of Venice's buildings and façades. However neither the composition nor the proportions are convincing. The frontage has been conceived as a single entity, with a central pedimented centre-piece forming a part of the cornice, over a largely undecorated frieze. Further down the building there is a pair of pilasters, featuring capitals of the Ionic order (a Greek design which originated in the sixth century B.C.), typically decorated with scrolls and ovolo *(see enlarged pillar left)* which are placed on fluted shafts. The pilasters are purely ornamental, giving the impression of a square column built into the wall. The treatment of heavily banded masonry pilasters above and the quoins to the sides of the façade is known as 'rustication'. Ordinarily it is found at the base of classical and neoclassical buildings. The building has clearly been designed to demonstrate the importance of the business in Winchester's commercial centre, but sadly the original shop front has long since been lost.

▲

Andrea Palladio was an Italian Renaissance architect who did most of his work in Venice and northern Italy. He was very influenced by classical Greek and Roman architecture. He is considered one of the most influential individual in the history of Western architecture.

The Winchester Co-operative Society purchased the building and had the façade re-built in 1910. By 1936 the Co-op included bakers, drapers, silk mercers, coal merchants, retail grocers, tea dealers, china and glass merchants, shoemakers and tailors - all under one roof. Seen here is the butcher's of the society located in nearby Jewry Street. The co-operative ceased to function in 1953. ▶

Photo: Hawkins Collection

The church of Il Redentore in Venice built after the plague of 1575 is a very good example of Palladian architecture. ▶

141 - 142, High Street

Built:	1921
Materials:	Brick
Original purpose:	Sainsburys Store
Key feature:	Pedimented balcony

The design of this building is a good example of promoting the importance of a business within its commercial setting. It combines neo-Georgian and neoclassical architecture and has as its central features the pediment and balcony, and the pilasters supporting the cornice. In fact this building was always meant to provide a strong corner to the junction of the High Street and Middle Brook Street *(see picture on page opposite)*. The original projecting canopy and shop front has been lost as has the original J. Sainsbury motif to the side.

As with many buildings of this period, the main feature of the building is supposed to look like expensive stonework, but by the 1770's the construction industry had started to make castings of great intricacy. In this case, the ornaments have been made with a cast using Portland cement - not carved stone.

Cheltenham & Glouceste

Numbers 141 and 142, High Street were, until 1921, probably the two oldest houses in Winchester. Like the Pentice (*see page 28*), they were medieval structures with overhanging upper stories. They were demolished in order to widen the road and the site was sold to an unassuming, publicity-shy businessman who wanted to build a shop and warehouse. This businessman was John James Sainsbury, founder of J. Sainsbury's, one of the biggest supermarket chains in the world. By 1921 J. Sainsbury's was already a chain of shops selling mostly dairy products. By the turn of the century there were five departments: dairy; bacon and hams; poultry and game; fresh meats,

'Keep the shops well lit'
Last words of J. Sainsbury's before his death in 1928

and cooked meats (including ox tongue in a jar - yum!). Although it was a far cry from the modern concept of a 'supermarket', J. Sainsbury's had already introduced many innovative ideas. From about 1890 every shop front was practically identical. This was so that clients could identify it quickly - a new marketing concept in those days! The interior design was also important: The shops were invariably long with an open corridor in the middle, which gave plenty of space to display food along the counters and walls.

Like everywhere else in Britain, when World War II broke out, rationing became an important part of life in Winchester. By 1940 every man, woman and child had a ration card, ensuring that each

individual had a fair share of the available food and could only purchase at a designated shop. Food didn't completely cease to be rationed until 1954. By 1964 the concept of 'supermarket' had kicked in and J. Sainsbury's had to move its business to a more appropriate premises just around the corner on Middle Brook Street - but far less interesting.

© The Sainsbury Archive, Museum of London Docklands

◄ **Sainsbury's opened on Winchester's High Street in 1922 and remained there for 42 years. This view is from 1959.**

▲ **A basket of basic goods during war and post-war rationing. Many products came from the USA - including dried eggs.**

23, High Street

Built:	1857 Grade II Listed
Materials:	Gault brick and stone
Original purpose:	Market
Key feature:	Doric columns

The architecture of 23, High Street is directly influenced by classical architecture, which had five orders: Tuscan, Doric, Ionic, Corinthian and Composite, described by the design of the columns. The column is composed of a base, a shaft and a capital at the top. In this case when we look at the columns it is immediately apparent that the building belongs to the Doric Order because they have a relatively plain capital and fluted shafts (unlike the similar earlier Tuscan order, which always has plain shafts). In addition the composition also shows a plain architrave and a frieze consisting of alternating Triglyphs (a feature of the frieze, intended to reflect timber construction), Metope (the square space between two Triglyphs) and laurel wreaths.

This building was clearly an expensive one to construct as, unlike many other examples within the city, the architectural details described here have been constructed in stonework.

"The gabled brick, tile, and freestone houses had almost dried off for the season their integument of lichen, the streams in the meadows were low, and in the sloping High Street, from the West Gateway to the mediaeval cross, and from the mediaeval cross to the bridge, that leisurely dusting and sweeping was in progress which usually ushers in an old-fashioned market-day."

- *Thomas Hardy from Tess of the D'Ubervillles.*

That's how Thomas Hardy sees Winchester's High Street in the final, and tragic, scene of his novel, Tess of the D'Ubervilles. On market-days Winchester must have been a hive of activity and the corner of the High Street and Market Street was the hub of all the excitement — and had been for

centuries. By the time the Normans arrived, Market Street already had its name. But Winchester's history as a market town goes back much further. In fact, Venta Belgarum, the Romans' name for Winchester, was set up as a market town in the first century A.D. and it is quite likely that the old Iron Age settlement occupied by the Romans had also been a centre of commerce. With hundreds of years of tradition, the idea of building Market House seemed a good one. It was built in 1857 on the site of what had previously been the Fleshambles — or meat market. At a cost of £1200, City Engineer William Coles built it in the Greek Doric revival style. Despite the classical design, it had the very modern feature of a glass roof and room for about 50 stalls.

One can't help thinking that Thomas Hardy must have been looking at Winchester with a rather romantic view because by the time "Tess" was published in 1892, market days were regarded as rather a nuisance

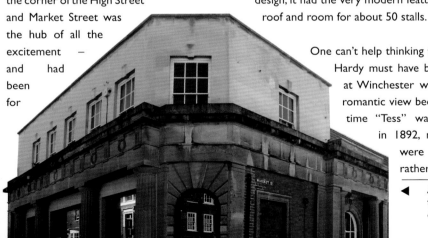

Sixteenth century market meat stall by Pieter Aertsen ▲

and Market House was in deep financial trouble. People complained that the overspill from the stalls onto the adjoining streets "interfered materially" with the shops. It seems that by the end of the 19th century tastes and habits had changed because most people were shopping at shops — not at market stalls. By 1896 the market had gone and Market House was altered by Thomas Stopher to accommodate a new business: Dumper's Restaurant, which remained a feature of Winchester life until 1958 when Market House was redesigned and brick walls were built to fill-in the space between columns.

◄ *Although the purpose of this book is to 'look up', in this particular case the added first floor is very plain in comparison to the ground floor - best to 'look down'.*

27, High Street

Built:	Late 18th c. Grade II Listed
Materials:	Brick
Original purpose:	Clock makers
Key feature:	Flat rubbed brick arch

In Britain we take sash windows for granted, but they are actually unique to only Britain and less so Holland. The sliding sash window was probably invented by the British scientist, philosopher and inventor, Robert Hooke in around 1670, but others (particularly the Dutch) believe it may have originated in Holland. The first sash windows were seen in England in about 1680, when they were employed in large numbers on the famous Chatsworth House in Derbyshire. However, Vermeer's painting of 'The Milkmaid' dates back to 1658 and features what seems to be a sash window.

The 'sash' is the panel which holds the panes and slides up and down. The mechanism consists of over forty-five individually joined pieces of wood. To balance the window there is a pair of cast iron weights and associated pulleys, which stop the window from crashing down when it's raised. The mechanism is contained in hidden sash boxes contained inside the walls around the window frame (see *drawing on opposite page*).

The Sash Window

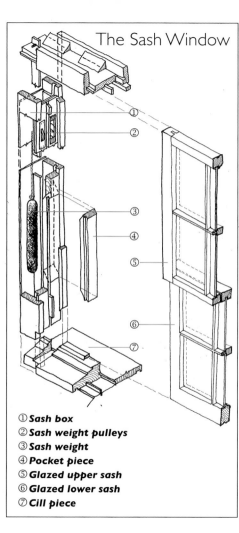

① **Sash box**
② **Sash weight pulleys**
③ **Sash weight**
④ **Pocket piece**
⑤ **Glazed upper sash**
⑥ **Glazed lower sash**
⑦ **Cill piece**

From 1830 to 1851 James Brown ran a clockmaking business, then his son, Henry, ran the business until 1861. Henry's brother, Edward, took over until 1886. Edward lived next door at number 26 with his wife, who was a milliner; his three children, and three servants. In 1871 Edward's son, Albert, joined the business. By 1886 the business was called E. Brown and Son and had expanded to include baby linen, carpet warehouse, corset maker, furrier, glover,. habit maker, hosier, shirt maker, linen draper, silk mercer, mantle maker, costumier, milliner, dressmaker, optician and . . . undertaker! It couldn't have been very successful because by the following year, 1887, the new occupier, William Thomas Salter, had reverted to being a watchmaker. He remained there until 1904 when Charles Spicer – yet another clockmaker - moved in and stayed there for 47 years. In 1951 Saunders and Co., jewellers and clockmakers, ran the business until 1985, when H Samuel, jewellers and clockmakers (of course), took over until 2003. Time and technology rolled on, and now the premises no longer sells clocks and watches, but mobile phones.

This building is exceptional because it has a very simple design, but at the same time the quality of its execution is excellent. The window detailing alone is impressive for two things: the arches forming the openings to the head of the windows and the proportion and construction of the windows themselves. Each window sits below a 'flat' arch of 'rubbed' bricks (above). The use of bricks to form arches is commonplace. However in this case each brick has been individually fired to a particular shape and then placed immediately against its neighbour without the use of mortar. The combined geometry of the bricks working together provides the essential bridging ability over the head of the window and the action of each brick surface against its neighbour provides sufficient friction for the bricks to be held in position.

118, High Street

Built:	1827, Grade II Listed Building
Materials:	Brick and stucco
Original purpose:	Stationer's, bookshop and public reading room
Key feature:	Stucco imitating coursed ashlar stone

At first glance, this building seems to be made of a very expensive material: stone. Coursed ashlar stone, to be precise. But if you look closely you will see that this is an illusion. In fact the building is mostly made of brick which has been rendered over and then 'drawn' using a traditional technique called stucco to give the impression of expensive ashlar stone at a much lower price! Stucco is a craft that is known to have been used since the early part of the 18th century, likely to be seen in England on some of the great renaissance buildings, made by the likes of Inigo Jones. Later, in the early 19th century, stucco was commonplace and widely used by John Nash in some of his fine London buildings, becoming a widespread treatment on building fronts across the country.

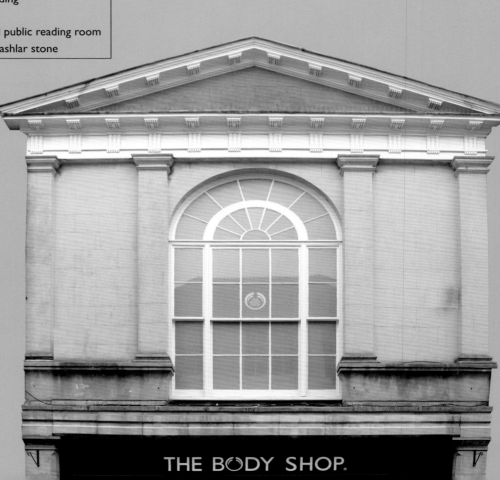

THE BODY SHOP.

▲ W T Warren, local historian and owner of Warren and Sons (see page 61), believed a Roman mint had stood on this site, but no evidence has yet been found.

118, High Street was built in 1827 and it served as a stationers, printers, book shop and public reading room – all rolled into one. It remained serving the same functions under three different owners for forty years. Then in 1867 it became a "corn and hay dealer".

The present building stands on the site of the Church of St. Mary Kalender. In fact, most of central Winchester was a part of the Parish of St. Mary Kalender. However by the 1640s it

had been abandoned, fallen into a terribly dilapidated state and was used as a place to dump offal by the local butchers. The stench must have been terrible! In 1652 the Plundered Ministers' Committee, set up by the parliamentarians, ordered that the church be closed and its parishioners attend St. Maurice's Church (which itself was mostly all pulled down in 1958, leaving only its Norman tower, on the High Street near Debenhams).

In the 1920's F.W. Woolworth purchased 118 to 121 High Street, demolishing everything but 118 in order to build one large store. Of course, to build it, they had to excavate to lay the foundations – a great opportunity for archaeologists! None was more enthusiastic than an amateur local archaeologist by the name of Sydney Ward-Evans. He wanted to communicate his knowledge and enthusiasm to the general public. Before there was an 'official' Winchester archaeologist, he led most of the local archaeological digs. He was particularly interested in Roman and Pre-Roman times and came up with the theory that there had been a Roman mint at the site. When excavating in 1929, they found a baptismal font, a 16th century well, a medieval carved stone and a Roman road.

▲ F.W. Woolworth shortly after conversion in 1930.

Sydney Ward-Evans in about 1930 showing the width of the City Wall at the ▼ Castle Avenue site.

31-35, High Street

Built:	About 1459 Grade II* Group Listed
Materials:	Oak timbers and infill brickwork
Original purpose:	Market stalls
Key feature:	Half-timbered

The vast majority of England's old timber framed buildings are of the mighty oak. Ordinarily the main timbers of a building were taken from trees specifically felled for use on that building and so most framed constructions were of green or unseasoned oak trunks and branches which were split or cleaved along their length to give the characteristic naturally curved appearance. Using green oak made it easier to work and

this was important because the joints had to be hand-tooled and then drilled and pegged at every junction. In fact the term for these buildings is 'half-timbered' because the main frames were in-filled with brick or mud to complete the elevation and also give lateral stability to the frame. These buildings are of a post-and-truss construction, which means that in general they display a means of supporting the roof rafters with a purlin in the line of the roof, which is itself supported on a timber truss.

Half-timbered houses were considered to be rather common and during the Georgian period in particular they would be over-clad in more 'expensive' materials such as brick to hide their original construction. It is clear that the timbers of no. 31, High Street are in fact a more recent attempt to mimmick the original architecture of 34 and 35, High Street.

This group of buildings is named "The Pentice", because of its covered walkway. William the Conqueror extended the Saxon Royal Palace destroying many houses and five "moneyors' mints". That left a blank wall along the High Street from the Butter Cross to Market Street. For centuries drapers and other stall holders had sold their wares in the middle of the High Street, so they merely moved up against the wall. As time went on the stalls became permanent buildings, extending further and further into the High Street. When the buildings could encroach no further without blocking the street, the upper floors were extended, creating the covered walkway. By the fifteenth century The Pentice was the city's cloth market and looked very much like it does today, with a small, narrow shop at the front and stairs leading to the private rooms above the shop and pentice.

In 1859 32, High Street was purchased by William Hayter, a china and glass dealer, who wanted to build a modern home for his business and family. To do the job, he hired Thomas Stopher, a well known Winchester architect. Mr. Stopher wanted to construct something in keeping with the other buildings, but he recounted that Mr. Hayter *"told me plainly if I was not prepared to build the house to his ideas, he would go to someone else who would!"* The result is plain to see.

▲ **Thomas Foster and his family occupied 34, High Street, from 1874 to 1979. He was a tobacconist and cigar importer. In 1980, when Fosters closed, the shop fittings and front were donated to the City Museum where they can still be seen.**

▲ **These are the original oak beams at 34, High Street, which have been carbon dated to 1459**

◄ **Odd one out. In about 1859 William Hayter decided to 'modernise' and rebuild one of The Pentice houses, defying planning laws and local opposition. Guess which!**

TIMPSON The Quality Service People

HENRY A. WHITE.

28

Photo: W T Green, c. 1903

29

113, High Street

Built:	1780, new façade 1937
Materials:	Brick and flintstone
Original purpose:	Inn
Key feature:	Knapped flint panels

Flint – knapped or unknapped – has been used from antiquity (for example at the Late Roman fort of Burgh Castle in Norfolk) to the present day as a material for building walls, using lime mortar and often combined with other available stone or brick rubble. It was most common in parts of southern England because there was no good building stone available locally and brick-making was not widespread until the later Middle Ages. It is especially associated with East Anglia, but also used in chalky areas stretching from Kent to Somerset. Flint was used in the construction of many churches, houses and other buildings, for example the large stronghold of Framlingham Castle. There are lots of decorative effects that can be achieved by using different types of knapping arranged with combinations of various stones (flushwork), which was particularly popular in the 15th and early 16th centuries.

THE WHITE HORSE INN

In the 19th century, The White Horse Inn was one of 23 pubs on Winchester's High Street. In 1808 its innkeepers were John Bell and his wife Sarah. At the time, Jane Austen, one of the most famous authors in the English language, was writing to her sister, concerning an issue that preoccupied her - adultery. She was writing about the uncomfortable situation of Colonel Thomas Powlett, a Southampton friend of the Austen family: "This is a sad story about Mrs. Powlett. I should not have suspected her of such a thing. A hint of it, with initials, was in yesterday's Courier; and Mr. Moore guessed it to be Lord Sackville, believing there was no other Viscount 'S' in the peerage, and so it proved".

According to the Hampshire Chronicle, "no private subject has so much occupied the attention of the neighbourhood, as this affair". What so much concerned Jane Austen and the Hampshire Chronicle was what had occurred at The White Horse Inn on 10 June 1808: Letitia Powlett, wife of Colonel Powlett, met her lover Charles Germain, Viscount Sackville for an amorous rendezvous. Unfortunately for them, they were spotted by Sarah Bell, the landlady. Later, during divorce proceedings, Sarah recalled that Letitia Powlett was shown to a "bedchamber on the second floor for an hour or two". After having breakfast on the ground floor, Charles Germain was shown to another bedchamber on the second floor. Lady Powlett's bedchamber "was and is number 4 and the bedchamber adjoining was and is number 3 and between the two chambers there was and is an intermediate door of communication". Sarah Bell spied on the couple from "an opposite chamber, numbered 2, from which she could view both doors of chambers numbered 3 and 4". This was the evidence presented by Sarah Bell at Winchester Diocese Consistory Court in 1809 during divorce proceedings between the Powletts.

Ironically, Charles Germain, Viscount Sackville, later the 5th Duke of Dorset, died in 1843 - unmarried, childless and both his titles became extinct.

The White Horse Inn closed in 1937 and the façade was rebuilt, but the sign was retained from the original building.

Jane Austen died in College Street, Winchester in 1817 and is buried at the Cathedral.

112, High Street

Built:	Mid -19th century
Materials:	London stock buff brick & ashlar stone
Original purpose:	Artist's studio
Key feature:	Corinthian capital

The big difference between this building and its neighbours is that the brick is yellow – more precisely, buff-coloured. The brick probably came from London, where the clay of the London Basin characteristically produces this light yellow colour. One can only suppose that the owner of this property chose a buff brick just to be different!

Additionally it borrows its capitals *(see page opposite)* from the Corinthian Order - the fourth of the five great classical orders *(see page 20)*. The Corinthian order is named after the Greek city where it originated in the 5th Century B.C. Later it was taken up by the Romans. The original design of the leaf-enfurled capital is said to have been influenced by a basket of toys placed on the grave of a young Corinthian girl, around which the acanthus plant had grown. The capitals themselves were probably cast from concrete, rather than carved from stone.

Richard Baigent (1799 - 1881) ▲

Richard Baigent senior was a well-known painter in Victorian England. He occupied this address as his home and studio between 1847 and 1871. According to the census of 1850, he was a drawing master, artist and stationer. When you see what the building looked like before being altered, it is clear that he used it as a studio with its large south-facing bay window allowing in a lot of light. He was assisted by his son, also named Richard, who was a water colourist and photographer. They were joined by Richard's younger brother, Francis Baigent, also an artist. Richard senior became the first Registrar for Winchester. After 1871 Francis and Richard shared the site with tailor, Benjamin Bear, until about 1882 when Richard junior emigrated to Canada, where he acquired a good reputation. Their work is today quite valuable.

▲ *Before alterations, there was a south-facing bay window*

◀ *Painting by Richard Baigent circa 1848 with Winchester College in the background. It can be seen at Winchester Museums.*

36 - 39, High Street

Built:	1908 Grade II* Group Listed
Materials:	Oak timbers and brick
Original purpose:	Chemist
Key feature:	Mock Tudor

You may be forgiven for thinking that this is an example of a superbly conserved medieval half-timber building like others in The Pentice, but you would be wrong. This is actually a superb example of high quality Edwardian 'Mock Tudor', which had been so fashionable in late Victorian times.

The building is an attempt by the owners to create a national identity for the Boot's brand (they built similar premises across the country), while still fitting-in with the character of the historic High Street. Boot's adopted the striking 'black and white' architecture that is associated with half-timbered buildings. However the timber is obviously of an engineered quality: straight and very evenly disposed on the elevation. In reality these timbers may be attached to a structural frame behind, which allows large windows to provide good internal lighting. To add to the effect, the glazing is mounted on leaded cames, common to medieval buildings (see page 49).

4 Bishops of Winchester

The four carved figures on the façade of the building represent some of the Bishops of Winchester.

Some of the clauses pertaining to the conversion of 38 - 39, High Street from residential to office premises set out by the County Architect in 1934 ▼

A.C. Roberts,
County Architect

1934

CONVERSION TO OFFICES OF 38 - 39 HIGH STREET

" . . . . all materials and articles used in the execution of the Contract shall be of British origin or manufacture . . . "

" . . . . allow £35-0-0 for contingencies . . . . "

" . . . . the cement is to be best English Portland, the sand to be river or pit sand, clean, sharp, of an approved quality . . . "

" . . . . the timber is generally to be Swedish, approved, sound, dry, very heavy and close grained and seasoned, imported Redwood . . . "

" . . . . the hair to be best strong ox hair, long, sound, free from grease and dirty, throughly beaten and dry . . . "

◀ **William of Wykeham (1324-1404) was keeper of the privy seal and chancellor of England. He was the founder of New College, Oxford and Winchester College.**

▲ **Letter from Walkelin, Bishop of Winchester dated 1082 regarding the building of the cathedral.**

▲ **St Æthelwold (909-984) was leader of the monastic reform movement in Anglo-Saxon England. He was said to be as "terrible as a lion" to the rebellious, yet "gentler than a dove" to the meek.**

◀ **Richard Fox (c.1448-1528) was appointed by Henry VII. He had a great deal of influence not only on Henry VII, but on his son, Henry VIII, who employed him in diplomatic and matrimonial negotiations.**

35

110, High Street

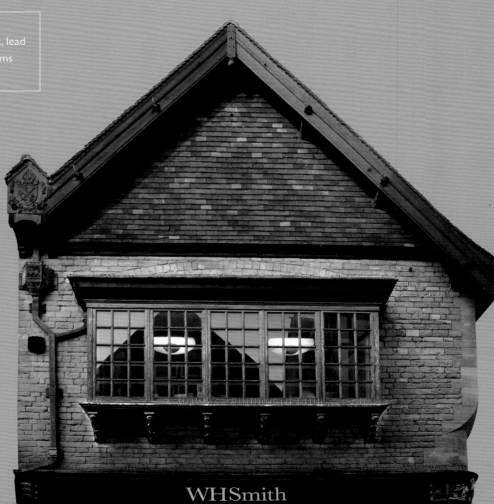

Built:	1927, Grade II Listed
Materials:	Timber, clay tiles, stone, oak, lead
Original purpose:	News vendor's and tea rooms
Key feature:	Arts and Crafts Influence

This building's composition and choice of materials makes it unique on the High Street: it brings together timber, clay tiles, two types of stone, decorative leadwork and oak-framed casement windows. Curiously, it is asymmetrical. The deliberate mix of materials and the composition of the façade shows that the architect wanted to create an Arts and Crafts building in the Domestic Revival Style, at a time when the Arts and Crafts Movement proper, had largely lost its foothold in England.

The materials are sensitively combined and used with an honesty and integrity that cannot be applied to the highly stylised 36-39, High Street (see page 34).

Note the low, wide-spanning brick arch that forms the opening to the projecting bay window. This arch is self-supporting and carries the weight of the gable above back to the stone walls at either side.

WHSmith

The man who built this building was George Blount, an architect based in Salisbury. His firm specialised in the style of Arts and Crafts and was responsible for many well-known buildings in southwest England, including churches and public buildings. He was 57 years old when W H Smith commissioned his firm to design and construct this building. He died 5 years later in West Grimstead, near Salisbury. George's younger brother, Clavell, was killed in the Battle of the Somme in 1916.

◄ *The current building runs from the High Street along Parchment Street to St. George's Street. In 1990 the hall of "Faith and Confidence" Masonic Lodge that stood at this corner was demolished to extend W H Smith's, but the Masonic symbols were retained.*

▲ *The gargoyles are above the main entrance of the shop.*

◄ ▶

George Blount and his entry in the register of the Royal Institute of British Architects.

Blount. — GEORGE LEO W. BLOUNT, The Cottage, Winterbourne Earls, Salisbury; son of the late Lieutenant Clavell W. S. Blount, R.N.; born at Aldeburgh, Suffolk, March 2nd, 1870; educated at Christ's Hospital; member Royal Institute of Architects, Ireland. Architect, surveyor and civil engineer; articled pupil to H. Seaver, B.E. Architect and Civil Engineer, 1885-1901; served in Civil Department of War Office at Belfast, Plymouth and Salisbury Plain; practised in Atlantic Buildings, Waring Street, Belfast, 1896-1900; opened office in Salisbury, March, 1905. Married Kathleen, daughter of the late Christopher Strong Black, M.D. of Kilkinamurry, co. Down, and Belfast, Ireland.

37

40, High Street

Built:	1874 Grade II* Group Listed
Materials:	Brick, stone and 'burnt' brick
Original purpose:	Butcher's
Key feature:	Diapering

The patterns displayed on the gable end of this building are known as 'diapering'. It is a way of decorating large expanses of brickwork panels by creating geometric patterns, usually diamond or lozenge shaped, through the use of brick headers (the 'ends' of a brick), which are darker than the adjacent brickwork. The darker bricks are likely to be from the same material as their adjacent bricks, but are 'burnt' in the kiln. A typical brick is fired at about 900°C. If the temperature is increased to about 1200°C, the bricks turn a darker red, purple or grey.

Diapering originated in the days of King Henry VIII when the technology of using bricks for building became better understood. We can see examples of such brickwork on eminent buildings of that period, such as Hampton Court Palace.

vision express

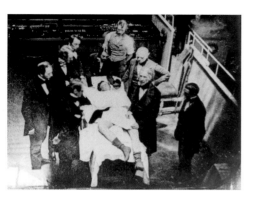

◄ *Daguerreotype taken in 1846, re-enacting a surgical operation before the days of sterile instruments - or anaesthesia. Note that the surgeons are wearing their normal street clothes.*

From 1819 to 1871 the premises were used as home, business and surgery. James Forder, a chemist, druggist and surgeon, ran his business there from the age of 28 to the age of 80. At that time, surgeons weren't necessarily trained in medicine. They mostly set bones, stitched wounds and pulled teeth, but they also extracted cysts or tumours - and they performed amputations. Joseph Lister didn't publish his findings on how to combat infection during and after surgical operations until 1869 so one can only assume that James Forder must have operated in the unhygienic conditions typical of the age. Perhaps it is somewhat of an irony that for the following 70 years no. 40, High Street was a butcher's: First, Henry Goodall from 1873 and 20 years later Howard Elkington until 1942. Elkington became Mayor of Winchester in 1913.

▲ *Howard Elkington, butcher and Mayor of Winchester in 1913.*

◄ *Number 40, High Street in about 1880, when it was Goodall's Butchers - note the carcasses hanging outside.*

39

The Market Cross or 'Buttercross'

Built:	15th c. Grade II Listed
Materials:	Stone
Original purpose:	Memorial
Key feature:	Original statue of St. John the Evangelist

Winchester's Market Cross is believed to have been erected in the fifteenth century. Standing at forty three feet high, it is considered to be the finest in the country. Sadly, only the Statue of St. John the Evangelist on the south side is original, the others were replaced during restoration work in 1865 carried out by Sir George Gilbert Scott. This was necessary because so much of the stonework had decayed very badly – only St. John the Evangelist was protected from the elements. In fact, we are lucky to have the Buttercross today at all. In 1770 a county magnate claimed the cross as his own and wanted to move it to his property at Cranbury Park. He hadn't counted on the determination of the people of Winchester, however. When his workmen arrived with winches and ropes to remove it, the populace drove the workmen out of the city in protest!

The name 'Buttercross', stems from the fact that market traders used to display the butter they had for sale on the steps of the cross.

There is a curious link between the four images on this page. Sir George Gilbert Scott restored Winchester's Buttercross and he is the designer of a great many Victorian churches and landmarks, including the Albert Memorial in Hyde Park. Sir George was a contemporary of the celebrated novelist Anthony Trollope (in fact they both attended Harrow at the same time). Trollope was a multitalented man who, in 1860, while working for the Post Office, designed the pillar post box, which is still seen throughout the country. The red pillar post box was the inspiration for the famous red telephone kiosk and the red telephone kiosk was designed in 1936 by Sir Giles Gilbert Scott, grandson of Sir George!

The Albert Memorial, designed by Sir George Gilbert Scott. ▲

The red telephone kiosk, one of the most famous icons of Great Britain, was designed by Sir Giles Gilbert Scott, grandson of Sir George Gilbert Scott, who restored the Buttercross ◀

▲ *The red pillar post box, designed by Anthony Trollope, was already a feature at Winchester's Buttercross in the 1870's when this picture was taken.* ▶

43

103 - 104, High Street

Built:	1881
Materials:	White brick
Original purpose:	Draper's
Key feature:	French influence

L.K.BENNETT

This rather splendid building looks a bit out of place in Winchester – it has more of a 'continental' look than the rest of the street. Why? Because it's composed of design elements from the French Renaissance and from Greek Classicism. A clue to the architect's intentions is given in the use of the head of the Greek god Zeus. Zeus's head is accompanied by a row of column capitals of the Corinthian order. The Temple of Zeus, completed

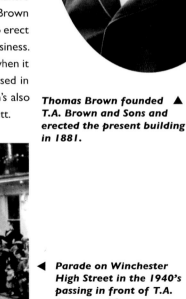

Zeus . . . probably

by Hadrian in 2 AD displayed a huge statue of Zeus and comprised Corinthian capitals. A number of these same capitals were removed by the Roman general Sulla during a visit in 40 AD and carried back to Rome, after which the Corinthian capital became a commonly used feature in Roman architecture. Zeus played many roles in people's imaginations and it is possible that this one is 'Zeus Argorias', keeping watch over business dealings at the market place – "agora" in Greek.

Before the present building there stood a three-storey structure, which had for generations been a drapers. In 1861, continuing with the tradition, Thomas Brown moved-in and set up T.A. Brown and Sons – drapers. As the business grew, it expanded its range of products and services. At its height they offered baby linen, carpet warehouses, corset makers, dyers' agency, furriers, glovers, habit makers, hosiers, shirt makers, linen drapers, silk mercers, mantle makers and costumiers, millinery, dressmakers and . . . undertakers! In 1881, Thomas Brown demolished the previous building in order to erect the present one as his family home and business. And so it remained in the family until 1953, when it became Plummer Roddis Ltd, in turn purchased in 1973 by Debenhams's. Curiously, Debenham's also started life as a draper's. It is now L.K. Bennett.

Thomas Brown founded ▲ T.A. Brown and Sons and erected the present building in 1881.

◀ **Parade on Winchester High Street in the 1940's passing in front of T.A. Brown and Sons.**

43

46 - 47, High Street

Built:	1806 Grade II Listed
Materials:	London Stock Buff Brick
Original purpose:	The White Hart Inn
Key feature:	First to use yellow London bricks

This building remains one of the city's finest Georgian buildings and it was responsible for bringing London Stock Buff brickwork to Winchester for the first time. Interestingly the building is designed as a single entity, yet it is actually two buildings separated centrally. The building incorporates a two-storey high arched centre window embellished with Greek columns of the Ionic order (similar to those which can be found at 7 - 8, High Street).

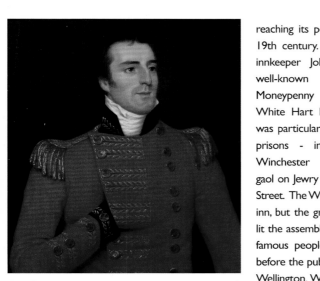

The Duke of Wellington ▲

reaching its peak in the late 18th and early 19th century. During its heyday, in 1806, innkeeper John Bell commissioned the well-known architect George Moneypenny to rebuild the White Hart Inn. Moneypenny was particularly famous for his prisons - including Winchester gaol on Jewry Street. The White Hart was popular not only as an inn, but the great main window on the first floor lit the assembly rooms providing a great venue for famous people, royalty and politicians to appear before the public. Amongst them was the Duke of Wellington. When campaigning for election as an MP he gave a speech from the first floor balcony. The life of the new White Hart Inn was short-lived however. The advent of the train meant the downfall of coaching inns and the White Hart closed its doors in 1857. As an ironic footnote, George Moneypenny, famous for his gaol houses, was himself unluckily incarcerated for debt – in one of his own gaols!

The White Hart Inn was first recorded in 1417. In those days the 'inn' was a fairly newfangled idea. Taverns and alehouses had been around for a long time as places for the locals to gather, much as we do today, for a sociable drink. The inn, however, provided not only the ale, but also food and accommodation for the ever increasing numbers of travellers, which were no longer merely the odd pilgrim passing through but also for commercial travellers. The inn, particularly the coaching inn, became more and more important and grandiose,

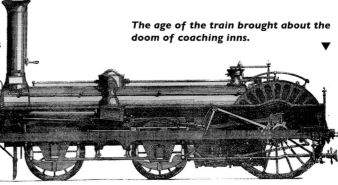

▲ *The age of coaching brought about the boom of coaching inns.*

The age of the train brought about the doom of coaching inns. ▼

49 High Street

Built:	1712, Grade II* Listed
Materials:	Brick with stone quoins and moulded stone cornice
Original purpose:	Court of law
Key features:	Clock and statue of Queen Anne

Anna Regina
Anno Pacifico
1713

Although it is known as The Old Guildhall, 49 High Street is not thought to have been the ancient meeting place of the Corporation, but a building used since 1349 as a hall of court where the Mayor of Winchester and the two bailiffs heard cases. The building was radically altered in Tudor and Stuart times and was almost demolished. However, it was rebuilt and refaced in 1712 and then extensively remodelled in 1915 by Thomas Stopher in order to house the present bank.

The main two exterior features of the building were the product of an intense rivalry between Winchester's two Members of Parliament at the time: George Brydges presented the city with the gift of a statue of Queen Anne, while, not to be outdone, Lord William Powlett donated the City Clock. The clock's face was the first in southern England to be lit by gas. The curfew bell in the bell tower (near the clock in the picture), still sounds at 8:00 p.m. each evening. The curfew was the time to extinguish all home fires until the morning. The clock projects over the street on a wooden bracket, but the mechanism and bell is actually in the copula above the building.

Queen Anne, 1702 - 1714 ▲

Thomas Hardy visited Winchester a number of times, both in his writing and in person. In the climactic chapter of Tess of the d'Urbervilles, Angel Clare and Eliza-Louisa leave Wintoncester through the Westgate and begin the long ascent out of town on their return to Dorset. As they reach the first milepost they hear the city clock ring eight, the curfew, and they turn to behold the city spread out below them. Their eyes do not latch onto the towers of the cathedral or Winchester College, or the spire of St Thomas's church, but on a *'large squat red-brick building with level grey roofs and rows of short barred windows'* – the prison. A few minutes past the hour a black flag is hoisted up the prison's flagstaff. It is the signal which announces Tess's execution.

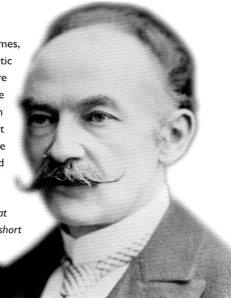

City Clock donated to Winchester in ▲
1713 by Lord William Powlett.

◀ **Thomas Hardy, author of 'Tess of the D'Urbervilles'. Tess's execution is signalled by the curfew bell of the City Clock in "Wintoncester" (Winchester).**

101, High Street

Built:	1462 Grade II* Listed
Materials:	Half-timbered
Original purpose:	Residence and chapel
Key feature:	Lead panel glazing

This half-timbered building includes a jettied façade, where the elevation is pushed out on timber brackets at each floor level. Though restored in 1958, the windows have kept the diamond pattern that would have featured in the original building of 1462. The windows consist of wooden casements that carry lead glazing bars called 'cames' within which diamond shaped glass pieces are held. Later seventeenth century equivalents would be similar in construction but would consist of rectangular glass panes. The lead cames and glass pieces would all be stiffened with cast iron rods to which the windows would be fixed with wire. These were be the equivalent of modern day glazing mullions designed to resist the pressure of wind on the window front. This type of window adds a particular character to a building's exterior appearance, while the interiors are significantly affected by the small areas of glass and comparatively large areas of lead cames.

'The glaziers' work before substantial was
I must confess, thrice as much lead as glass,
Which in the sun's meridian cast a light,
As it had been within an hour of night'.

- from the poem, "The Wonders of the Peake" by Charles Cotton (1630-1687)

Godbegot House is a corruption of Godbegeaton or, in modern English, "Good Bargain". In 1012 King Ethelred the Unready granted his queen, Emma of Normandy, an estate in Winchester, which included a private residence, a chapel, and a tenement known as Ælfric's Godbegeaton. When Queen Emma died, she bequeathed it to the Priory of St. Swithun. This caused a lot of problems - serious social problems. Why? Because at that time, this precinct measuring only 132 feet by 148 was not bound by the city's authorities. It held its own courts under the Steward of St. Swithun's Priory - the Cathedral. 'Evildoers' could commit crimes and take refuge in Godbegot Manor and there was nothing the Mayor or his city officers could do about it. It was particularly galling because this refuge was right in the middle of a busy city and easily accessible to the criminals. Finally with the Reformation, Godbegot went to the Dean and Chapter, losing it invulnerable status in the process.

Not mock Tudor. Before the 18th century it was very difficult to produce large panes of glass. They had to make a lot of small ones. Each 'diamond' is a pane of glass, held together by strips of lead, called "glazing bars or lead cames". ▲

King Ethelred the Unready granted his wife, Queen Emma of Normandy, an estate and residence in Winchester - the Manor of Godbegot ▲

The building as it stands today was built in 1462. According to Tom Atkinson, in his book 'Elizabethan Winchester', " . . . in 1471 it was described as timber-frame construction with wattle and plaster infill. By 1649 it was described as made of timber with 'Flemish Wall' (brick infill) and tile roof. There were four tenements fronting onto the High Street of which two survive. The ground floor rooms served as shops with two or three floors of private accommodation above, and at least one had a cock croft in the attic".

The building was almost demolished in 1938, but the City Council intervened,

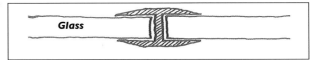

▲ *Glazing Bar or Lead Came*

purchasing it under the Town and Country Law for £8000. Since then the Council has been careful to ensure that certain features are maintained by new lessees. One business called Bernfield Brothers wanted to lease the premises, but no plain glass window could substitute the diamond-shaped glazing bars. Bernfield Brothers decided that *"the premises would not be suitable for our trade, your suggestion of leaving the existing mullions and transoms would be hopeless, as these would only obstruct any window display"*.

51-52, High Street

Built:	1883
Materials:	Brick, stone, timber, render
Original purpose:	Public house
Key feature:	Dolphin heads

From the late 19th to the 20th century there was a vogue for the Tudor Revival style, or, more commonly, 'Mock Tudor'. The original Tudor style refers, of course, to the period from about 1485 to 1600 when the Tudors (such as Henry VIII and Elizabeth I) reigned in England. The Revival was harking back to a time of simplicity represented by the Elizabethan cottage, where the family gathered in front of the warmth of the hearth and had their meals at a large, wooden table. Today, that style of architecture is regarded by many as bad taste. But when Thomas Stopher built this 'half-timber' structure (*see facing page*), it was an appropriately fitting design.

ceased to be a pub when in 1981 its 100-year lease ran out. The *Southern Evening Echo* wrote at the time: *"The closing of the Dolphin is seen as another nail in the coffin, the dying of the heart of Winchester."*

There has been a pub called 'The Dolphin' at this site since at least medieval times. With the passage of time, several buildings housing the Dolphin have been built and demolished. However, the name and nature of the building remained the same. The building prior to the present one was distinctive as one of the very few in Winchester to be made of stone. It was demolished in 1882 for the current building to be designed and erected by Thomas Stopher. It remained a pub at the very heart of Winchester's social life. In fact, in 1900, the Dolphin was one of twenty pubs on the High Street alone. That has all changed and the Dolphin

The Dolphin Inn (around 1870) was one of the few buildings in Winchester to be made of stone. ▼

Thomas Stopher ▲

Thomas Stopher was a prominent architect in Victorian Winchester responsible for many of the buildings and façades on the High Street. Born in London in 1837, he came to Winchester when he was very young. His father had been appointed County Surveyor in 1840. Stopher was educated at Trafalgar House School, and later trained as an architect and surveyor in his father's office. Eventually Stopher succeeded his father as surveyor to Winchester College and St John's Hospital.

Although an architect, Stopher had many interests and was very active in public life: In 1872 he was elected to Winchester City Council, by 1883 he was alderman and he served as Mayor of Winchester on three occasions, in 1876, 1883 and 1893. The portrait seen here is at Abbey House and depicts him wearing his Mayoral chain.

EASTON'S RESTAURANT

GUILDHALL WINCHESTER
CONCERT
TEST VALLEY
ON TUESDAY, MAY 25th 1897
TANNHAUSER OVERTURE
The SPECTRE'S BRIDE
180 PERFORMERS

53

98 - 99, High Street

Built: 1891
Materials: Terracotta, brick and stone
Original purpose: Shops
Key feature: Dutch gables and hanging tiles.

Originally the land where this building stands was a part of the tenement of Godbegot *(see page 48)*, The earliest reference to it is in the Domesday Book in the year 1110, where we are told that Adelwold, the King's Reeve of Winchester, built three properties on the King's road - the back of the building was the original frontage of the High Street.

In 1891, Thomas Stopher, a Victorian Winchester-based architect *(see page 51)*, renovated the façade of this building to incorporate Dutch gables and highly ornamental deep-red hanging terracotta tiles. 'Terracotta' . . . the word, taken from the Latin 'terra cocta', means 'fired earth'. However, the material, used to make these intricately shaped tiles is a carefully blended mixture of clay and sand, which has been hand-pressed in a mould, removed and then fired to a hardness that is seldom achieved with bricks. As the Latin name indicates the use of terracotta came from Italy and is first known to be used in England during Tudor times. The glazed version of this material more commonly found on brickwork in greens and whites is known as 'faience'. The tile forms used on this building

▲ **The goddess emerges from a scallop shell - 'The Birth of Venus' (circa 1486) by Sandro Botticelli.**

are known as 'scallops' - if you compare the stylised tiles to the actual scallop shell, you can see why. Scallop shells have been a part of art and architecture throughout history. Perhaps the most beautiful use of the scallop shell is in Botticelli's depiction of 'The Birth of Venus'. The ancient Greeks used a stylised scallop to fasten their tunics. Scallops were used in coats of arms, which made reference to ancestors who had been in the Crusades. They are also a symbol used by Christians undertaking pilgrimage as the means of taking drinking water from a vessel.

◄ **Dutch gable with stylised scallop-shaped hanging tiles.**

55 - 56, High Street

Built:	1913
Materials:	Brick, timber and render
Original purpose:	Picture House
Key feature:	Decorated raised lead panelling

This building was commissioned by a Mr A. Schomberg, specifically for use as a picture house and tea rooms and was designed by architects Stansfield Greenwood of Southampton. At that time the building featured an orchestra pit, as the 'talkie' (talking movie) had not yet been introduced.

The picture house operated here between 1914 - 1929, when it was taken over by Winchester Picture House Limited in 1930 and it continued to operate as a cinema and cafe with a capacity of 450 seats up to 1936. In this year, the first 'talkie' was presented here. It was operated in its final year by Odeon Theatres Limited before its ultimate closure and conversion to other uses.

▲ **Window detail from Glasgow School of Art by C. Rennie-Mackintosh (1909)**

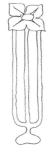

▲ **Raised plant detail in lead panelling.**

The elevation of the building is hardly noteworthy except for the fact that it contains a mild reference to the Art Nouveau movement, which had largely ceased in England by the time this building was completed in 1913. The movement was epitomised by the use of plant-inspired motifs, often stylised to accentuate their fluid linear qualities. The drawing (above right) is of the raised motif which can be seen on the high level lead panels between bay window openings. The question is, did the architects intend any reference? Certainly the square leaded windows hold a similarity to those used by Art Nouveau architect Charles Rennie-Mackintosh in his Glasgow School of Art completed in 1909 (above left), Could this be Winchester's only attempt at an Art Nouveau building?

◄ **'Shock Punch' (1925) was the film playing at the time this photo was taken.**

Extract from a review of 'Shock Punch' by Mordaunt Hall in 'The Screen' magazine, 11 May 1925:

A Hollywood conception of Scotsmen who wear the kilt but whose complexions betray nary a sign of the ruddy ruggedness due to Highland rain and wind is to be seen at the Capitol this week in a picture called "The Sporting Venus," which strange title, as a matter of fact, does give a "mon that is a mon" one wee chance to sound his burr. Robert Burns wrote:

"O wad some pow'r the giftie gie us To see oursels as ithers see us?"

The answer comes from California, and it is a question whether the Wallaces, the Bruces, the Watts and the McTavishes will smile with any satisfaction upon it. Not that they are intentionally maligned in this story, but that the men from the land of the heather are portrayed with studio-blanched complexions and, in one or two instances, wearing brocaded silk dressing gowns. Marshall Neilan, the director of this celluloid effusion, in his desire to depict Lady Grayle as a plucky person at the eleventh hour of a fast life, shows her ladyship smoking a cigarette before she breathes her last.

Built: 1935
Materials: Brick
Original purpose: Hotel
Key feature: Headless Black Swan

The Black Swan. The overhanging upper part must, of course, be of timber, and is probably Elizabethan; it is carried on a brick ground storey. An early ninteenth century remodeling, not without a certain massive dignity. It has a good sign showing us what that *rara avis*, a black swan, is really like."

- *Winchester Street Architecture, by T.D. Atkinson, Architect, 1934*

SOUTHGATE ST

HARVEY JONES   KITCHENS   HARVEY JONES   HARVEY JONES

65, The High Street was formerly the site of the 18th century Black Swan Hotel, an "inn of some repute". Evidently, one of its most noted guests was Sir Arthur Conan Doyle who stayed there in 1882 while researching for his short-story, *The Adventure of the Copper Beeches,* featuring Conan Doyle's legendary fictional detective, Sherlock Holmes. The original series of buildings, which formed the Black Swan Hotel were demolished in 1935 to improve the High Street – Southgate Street junction. The replacement, although bland in appearance, retains the only original feature of the building; a timber carved black swan, the head of which was lost and which is yet to be replaced.

Enlarged detail of the The Black Swan taken 1870 (see right). Note the suspended gaslight below the bunch of grapes. This is now also missing. ▶

'The Adventure of the Copper Beeches'
by Sir Arthur Conan Doyle, *Strand Magazine (1892)*

A Miss Violet Hunter contacts Sherlock Holmes to ask for his advice. She has been offered a 'situation' by a Mr Jephro Rucastle to act as the governess to his young son. The post is highly paid. However, it is offered with some suspiciously unusual conditions attached. She must have her hair cut short and on occasions must wear a specific blue dress when asked to do so. She needs the money but she wants Mr Holmes to know of her place of work, namely: 'The Copper Beeches' a country house five miles from Winchester, in case the suspicious nature of her employment has a more sinister side.

A fortnight later Mr Holmes receives a telegram:

▲   **Sir Arthur Conan Doyle**

"Please be at the 'Black Swan' Hotel at Winchester at midday to-morrow. Do come! I am at my wit's end. Hunter"

Mr Holmes and his faithful assistant Watson attend as requested and discover the villainous truth behind Mr Rucastle's employment of Miss Hunter . . . .

Black Swan around 1870 - when the swan still had its head ! ▼

Advertisement for the Black Swan, 1868 ▼

Photo: W. Savage

85, High Street

Built:	1836 Grade II Listed
Materials:	Brick
Original purpose:	Publishers and stationers
Key feature:	Bricked up windows

The one most noticeable thing about this building is that out of its ten windows, five have been bricked-up. Why . . . ? Possibly because of the Window Tax. In 1696 there was no such thing as income tax, but King William III wanted to tax people according to their wealth. At that time glass was very expensive, so the logic was that the more windows you had, the more wealth you had, and the wealthier you were the more you could be taxed. It was a very unpopular tax which, with many houses becoming virtually windowless, led to squalid living conditions. It was revoked for a short time, but had to be brought back to boost the coffers to finance the war against Napoleon. The tax was finally repealed in 1851.

Warren and Son is the oldest business on Winchester High Street. It was founded in 1835 by Nathaniel Warren as a printers and publishers, but at that time their premises were on Parchment Street. This building was used as the local courthouse and also housed Winchester's prison governor. The prison was on Jewry Street (now the Old Gaol House public house), and there was an underground passage that allowed the convicted prisoners to be taken straight from the court to the gaol to start their sentences.

Warren & Son moved here in about 1850 and William Thorn Warren (the 'son' in Warren and Son) took over the business in 1866 when his father died. The company continued to publish very successful books and guides and expanded the business to include the 'Hampshire Observer', a newspaper that had been owned by Lord Northbrook. W. T. Warren was not only a businessman, but also a well known amateur historian, particularly interested in Roman Winchester *(see his map of Roman Winchester on page 27).*

▲ *Warren's Guide to Winchester was published from 1836 to 1954. WT Warren also wrote several books on Winchester history.*

There was an underground passage leading from 85 High Street when it was a courthouse to the prison on Jewry Street. The central part of the building is now a public house. All but the central part and the north wing have been demolished.

▶

This quill and pen sign hung outside Warren & Son until very recently. It is made out of solid oak and was carved locally in the 1980s. It is currently being restored.

▲

The Westgate

Built:	c. 1220 Grade I Listed
Materials:	Stone
Original purpose:	Defensive wall
Key feature:	Five machicolations

From Roman times, when Winchester was known as Venta Belgarum, the city had a protective wall surrounding it (the only surviving part of that Roman wall can be seen just south of Bridge Street on the River Itchen). When the Romans left, the Saxons built another wall and then the Normans built yet another in the twelfth century and added bits, renovating it until the fifteenth century. The Westgate is a part of that wall. In those days there were five gates, through which to access the city. Eastgate, Southgate and Northgate were demolished in the 17th century, but King's Gate and Westgate still survive.

▲ *Five machicolations through which molten lead was poured onto invading armies.*

Outside the Westgate there was a deep ditch which was crossed using a drawbridge. The raising chains came out of the mouths of the two gargoyles visible on the outside of the gate on either side of the coats of armour. Additional protection was afforded by 5 machicolations just above the main entrance through which melted lead or boiling tar was poured down onto the would-be invaders below. With the invention of gunpowder two gun ports were added for the use of handheld cannons.

▲ *The Westgate in about 1870. Today the road goes around the gate, through what was then the "Plume of Feathers' public house.*

During the English Civil War of 1135 - 1154, King Stephen besieged the Empress Matilda at Winchester – it became known as the "Rout of Winchester". What happened was that the Bishop of Winchester fell out with Matilda and his army took refuge in Wolvesey castle. So

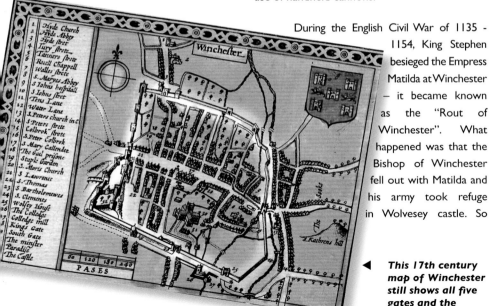

◄ *This 17th century map of Winchester still shows all five gates and the surrounding wall.*

Matilda occupied Winchester and laid siege to the castle. Cleverly, Stephen's army surrounded Winchester. Consequently a strange situation existed where there was an army in Wolvesey castle under siege from an army in the town, which itself was under siege from another army outside the walls! The last time the Westgate served its defensive purpose was during the English Civil War when Winchester was stormed by Oliver Cromwell in 1645. After that the Westgate became a city prison. Shackles on the first floor suggest that it was a place of torture and execution. Today we are a little less barbaric . . . the Westgate is now a lovely museum !

Acknowledgements:

For their support, encouragement and practical help, the authors wish to express their gratitude to:

Winchester City Council
In particular:

Ellen Simpson (Tourism and Marketing)
Alison Davidson (Historic Environment)
Marilyn Michalowicz (Arts Development)
Pru Hatton - For the supply of photographs (Economic and Cultural Services – Museums)
Ross Turle - For the supply of photographs and advice (Economic and Cultural Services – Museums)

For their advice and assistance:
Andrew Rutter RIBA
Dr Tom James PhD (Emeritus Professor, University of Winchester)
Dr Mark Allen PhD (University of Winchester)

For their co-operation:
Sainsbury's PLC
The National Trust
The George Roger Brown Collection

For her excellent source of information:
Dr Justine Cooper PhD
("Aspects of the Development of Winchester's High Street, 1550 - 2000...")

For their excellent services:
Hampshire County Council Records Office
Wiltshire Council, Department of Communities, Libraries, Heritage and Arts

About the authors

Christopher Newberry is a freelance writer, designer and photographer who has worked as a producer and director of television documentaries and educational radio. He shares his life with Frances and their children, Luke and Pablo.
www.thelot-media.co.uk

Rodney Graham is a practising architect and one of the founding directors of Design Engine Architects. He was born and has lived in Winchester most of his life. He is married to Paula, with whom he has three children - Ellery, Lawson and Bronte.
www.designengine.co.uk

Christopher and Rodney have combined their interests and skills to produce an original visual perspective focusing on the relation between architecture, social history and high street environments to create the *Look Up!* series.
www.lookup-winchester.co.uk

Working with